Lord Byron and Lady Caroline Lamb

Mad, Bad And Dangerous To Know: The Passionate and Public Affair That Scandalised Regency England

by

Joanne Hayle

Lady Caroline – 1785 to 1812

Lady Caroline was born on the 13th November 1785.

She was the only daughter of the Viscount and Viscountess

Duncannon, Frederick (1758-1844) and Henrietta (1761- 1821)

Ponsonby.

In 1793 they became the third Earl and Countess of

Bessborough.

Between 1785 and 1793 Caroline was titled The Honourable

and after her parent's status changed she became Lady

Caroline.

She had two elder brothers. John was born in 1781 and

Frederick in 1783. William followed in 1787.

Bessborough House in Roehampton, London, close to

Richmond Park, the largest royal park in the city, had been

built for Frederick's father William Ponsonby, the second Earl

of Bessborough .

Caroline's mother was known as Harriet to her family and friends, she was the second daughter of the first Earl and Countess Spencer who resided at Althorp House in Northamptonshire. (Earl Spencer lived 1738-1783/the Countess 1737-1814.)

The first Earl Spencer's great grandfather had been John Churchill, the first Duke of Marlborough, and the Earl is also H.R.H. William, the Duke of Cambridge's great great great great great grandfather.

A recently widowed Lady Spencer stayed with the Bessborough's for ten days after Caroline's birth. Initially Caroline only slept well when she was with her grandmother in her bed.

With a petite frame, Caroline appeared rather delicate, she had blonde -red hair and freckles.

As she grew up it was noted that she had a lisp and that she used baby talk when she was no longer an infant. Her teeth were said to be excellent.

Caroline's paternal grandmother was Lady Caroline Cavendish, the wife of William Ponsonby since 1739. She was the 2nd Countess Bessborough.

Her paternal great aunt was Lady Elizabeth Cavendish, John Ponsonby's wife since 1743.

These Cavendish ladies were daughter's of the third Duke of Devonshire.

Georgiana, the famed fifth Duchess of Devonshire was Harriet's elder sister and therefore Caroline's aunt.

Other aristocratic names peppered Caroline Ponsonby's family tree, for example, the Duke of St. Albans, the Earls of Peterborough and Sunderland and the Viscount Mountmorres.

Through her enviable connections the young Caroline met George, Prince of Wales, later King George IV and several other European royal figures. The French Queen Marie Antoinette was an acquaintance of the family.

Frederick's behaviour towards his wife could be abominable, he publicly chastised her about her gambling debts, although he accrued enough of his own, and he neglected her as a husband.

Harriet took lovers including the playwright, politician and theatre owner Richard Brinsley Sheridan who on his deathbed expressed the wish that his ghost would haunt her.

She bore two illegitimate children, Harriet and George, by Lord Granville Leveson-Gower.

She concealed these pregnancies from her husband.

Leveson-Gower married her niece Lady Harriet (Harryo) Cavendish at her suggestion and with her blessing.

As she released her lover of seventeen years she acknowledged that he had possibly loved her less than the other men in her life whilst she had idolised him.

Luckily, Harryo enjoyed a happy marriage and had five surviving children.

Caroline lived in Italy between the ages of six and ten years old, she almost died there from a worm related illness, her recovery was painful.

Her mother's health seems to have had a heavy impact on the young Caroline's mind too, when she was seven years old Harriet became ill, spitting blood and experiencing spasms. This understandably panicked Caroline greatly and around the same time she experienced the deaths of a young boy and her grandmother's dog.

These events were met with great emotion, perhaps neurotically.

A special governess was employed to attend her when she was at her most troubled and in an effort to restore and maintain her peace of mind Caroline lived a secluded life there.

When the family returned to England she joined her cousins, William, the Marquess of Hartington, Lady Harriet (Harryo) and Lady Georgiana Cavendish for schooling at Devonshire House. Caroline was closest to Harryo.

Lady Elizabeth Foster's children including Caroline and Augustus, fathered by the fifth Duke of Devonshire, were taught with them.

Besides the home tutoring she attended the Dame School in Knightsbridge, London.

Caroline's emotional outbursts were seen as a reason to be ever more protective by her mother and Spencer grandmother. Caroline became wilful and difficult to manage as a result, she was harshly punished by her tutors but not by her relations and the boundaries for acceptable behaviour were not clearly defined.

Caroline claimed in later life that she had been unable to read or write until she was an adolescent.

This can be easily disproven, letters written by Caroline in 1796 serve as proof that she was ably literate and witty. Moreover, her education would not have been ignored by her Spencer grandmother, the daughter of a diplomat and philanthropist, Lady Spencer was greatly in favour of a rich education for girls as well as boys.

The children's governess, Selina Trimmer was the daughter of Sarah Trimmer, a highly respected author of the era.
Under Lady Spencer's guidance Miss Trimmer conducted a thorough teaching programme and from the age of six, perhaps seven years old, Caroline's education included French and Italian which she learned to speak fluently and to read well, Greek, Latin, music and drama.
The young Caroline sketched, wrote poetry and prose and showed a flair for humour and impersonations.
She was a self confessed tomboy.
Worryingly, it's believed that the adolescent Caroline experimented with the sedative laudanum.

Lady Caroline Ponsonby was given a traditional coming out ball in Paris in 1802.

That same year she met William Lamb, the first Viscount Melbourne's second son at Brocket Hall in Hertfordshire.

His mother Elizabeth (nee Milbanke, a surname that featured in Byron's later life) had orchestrated their introduction in the hope that a marriage and career advancement for her son would follow.

Happily, the couple found that they enjoyed one another's company, he was an atheist and she was religiously inclined and although they argued they were devoted to each other. He did not try to curb her wild tendencies.

William Lamb was born on 15th March 1779 but it was rumoured that his father was not Sir Peniston Lamb but George Wyndham, 3rd Earl of Egremont.

He was educated at Eton and Trinity College, Cambridge and he formed friendships with a number of the *romantics* including Percy Bysshe Shelley and Lord George Byron.

Despite William being a rising star in political spheres Caroline's parents were reluctant to let her marry.

He had been an admirer of Harriet's, his future mother in law, but it was Caroline's age and the bride and groom's personalities that caused concern.

However, permission was given and William and Caroline were married on 5th June 1805.

The Lamb's ancestral homes were Brocket Hall, an impressive neoclassical pile to the north of Hatfield in Hertfordshire and the extensive Melbourne Hall in South Derbyshire. Their Piccadilly home in London was called Melbourne House.

The Lamb's marriage started well, of note was the banquet that Caroline gave for her husband's birthday at Brocket Hall where she was "served" utterly naked to him in a silver dish in front of their guests.

After two miscarriages, Caroline bore a son George Augustus Frederick Lamb on 11th August 1807 and a daughter followed in 1809 but she sadly died within twenty four hours of her birth.

Their son suffered from mental health problems but they refused to adhere to the practice of the times and have him institutionalised, he was cared for at home.

Caroline suffered greatly throughout her pregnancies and in recovery from them. It's been said that her ill health was made worse by her husband's ardent attention in the bedroom.

His career prospered, in 1806 William was elected to the House of Commons and he held three different seats over the next six years.

Work commitments and the toll of their son's poor health put pressure on the marriage and this established a distance between them.

They endured emotional scenes and her passionate love affair with Sir Godfrey Vassal Webster.

William forgave her for the liaison although it caused embarrassment to the Lamb family.

Elizabeth, William's mother, came to dislike Caroline intensely.

A bored Caroline had deviated from the path of virtue and the society's rules once, her next great passion would be a far more public affair.

George Byron – 1788 to 1812

Byron was born on 22nd January 1788.

His parents were the Army Captain John "Mad Jack" Byron (1756-1791) and his second wife Catherine, nee Gordon (1770-1811,) the heiress to the Gight Estate and its sixteenth century castle in Aberdeenshire, Scotland.

Byron's father's first marriage had been to Amelia Osborne, Marchioness of Caermarthen. The Marchioness had divorced her husband to marry "Mad Jack," her lover.

She bore him two daughters but only one survived, Augusta Maria Byron.

Amelia died aged twenty nine on 27th January 1784, a year and a day after Augusta's birth; she'd been married for just under five years.

The infant Augusta was sent to live with her grandparents, Robert and Mary Darcy, the fourth Earl and Countess of

Holderness.

John was said to be a cruel man who married both of his wives for their fortunes. Amelia had possessed a £4000 per year income and Catherine had accrued a fortune of the then vast sum of £23000.

He married Catherine Gordon on 12th May 1785.
Her fortune was used to pay off his massive debts and after this her income was reduced to just £150 per year.
To avoid her husband's creditors Catherine accompanied him to the Isle of Wight and France but she returned to the English mainland in 1787 so that her child could be born in England.

The baby was christened at the St. Marylebone Parish Church in London.
George Gordon Byron was named after an ancestor, one of King James I of Scotland's descendants.

While John Byron waited to inherit his English title of Lord Byron in the Barony of Byron of Rochdale, he claimed his wife's Scottish estate.

He renamed himself John Byron Gordon and George was known as George Byron Gordon.

To pay off "Mad Jack's" gambling debts the estate was sold to George Gordon, the third Earl of Aberdeen for his son George, Lord Haddo, Byron's cousin.

In 1790 a depressed and deserted Catherine and two year old George moved in to simple lodgings in Aberdeenshire.

John Byron died in Northern France on 2nd August 1791 aged thirty five. It is likely that he died from tuberculocis although his son claimed that he had committed suicide.

The nine year old Byron was faced with the inappropriate attention of one of the caretakers at the lodgings, May (Mary) Gray. Allegedly, she used to go to bed with him and "play tricks with his person." She then used her abuse as a means to blackmail George in to silence when she was behaving badly and drinking heavily.

She was dismissed when he was eleven years old, apparently for beating him rather than the above behaviour.

It's believed that Catherine's paramour, a Lord Grey, made advances towards him too and it has been speculated that this might somehow account for Byron's future liaisons with adolescent males. He never disclosed anything to his mother although he refused to speak to Lord Grey.

Byron was attracted to two of his female cousins, Mary Duff, when he was eight, and later Margaret Parker.

George's great uncle William was the 5th Lord Byron, *"the wicked lord"* who died aged seventy five in May 1798.

William Byron had killed his cousin, Mr. Chaworth, in a duel and later his own coachman.

He subsequently fell in to a period of eccentricity that verged on madness. It led him to neglect the ancestral home, Newstead Abbey in Nottinghamshire, and he ruined the family fortunes to spite his son who'd married against his advice. The son, John, predeceased him by twenty two years.

It was William's ten year old great nephew's mixed fortune to accede to the title and estate and to take responsibility for the family debts with his mother's assistance. Such was the state of disrepair at Newstead Abbey that Catherine arranged for the property to be leased to third parties until George Byron was old enough to manage it.

Unfortunately Catherine drank too much and she was said to either overindulge her son or be foul tempered with him. An example of her ill humour was when she branded Byron, who was born with a club foot and very self conscious about it, "a lame brat."

Young Byron grew to mock rather than respect Catherine and he was reputedly disgusted by her alcohol consumption.

He attended Aberdeen Grammar School and Dr.William Glennie's school in Dulwich, London but his education was compromised by Catherine, she would periodically take him out of school and she interfered in what he was educated about with the result that George lacked broad knowledge in several areas and also discipline.

However, his keen interest in history and reading (he loved the Bible) would prove to be invaluable in his writing career.

Byron was athletic, swimming was his forte, he could box and horse ride well.

He was encouraged not to overwork his club foot by a Dr. Bailey but this advice was often ignored

He would wear several layers of clothing when he exercised so that he would perspire more and maintain his figure.

Byron was a vegetarian and he followed a strict diet, some days he'd only eat dry biscuits and occasionally he'd feast on meat and puddings before purging himself. This has led biographers to question if Byron had either of the eating disorders bulimia or anorexia.

Byron attended Harrow between 1801 and 1805, an esteemed public school in London that had been inaugurated by Queen Elizabeth I and founded by John Lyon, a wealthy farmer, in 1572.
While there he did not distinguish himself academically.

He met another of his cousins during his time there. Mary Chaworth was considered to be his first love.
In his memoirs he refers to her as the first girl that aroused his sexual feelings.
She was also the reason that he refused to return to the school

in 1803 although he relented and resumed his studies there in January 1804.

Upon his return he formed a passionate attachment to his fellow student, John Fitzgibbon, 2nd Earl of Clare.
He continued his studies at Trinity College, Cambridge, where he became involved with John Edleston. Byron referred to their affair as *"a violent, though pure love and passion."*
Edleston and Fitzgibbon were younger than Byron so perhaps his use of the word pure was a profession of innocence in an age when homosexuality was a crime that carried devastating penalties including being publically hanged.

Trinity College did not allow dogs and Byron was not allowed to have his beloved Botswain with him.
As an act of protest he sought a new pet, a tamed bear.
Bears weren't mentioned in the college's statutes so he could not be legally challenged about having one.

He even offered to apply for a college fellowship for his furry friend.

Time away from Harrow and Trinity College was spent with his mother in Nottinghamshire and during his visits he formed a friendship with brother and sister, John and Elizabeth Pigot. The trio staged plays together and they encouraged him to write poetry.

Byron's first volume *Fugitive Pieces* was successfully published but on the advice of another of his friends, Reverend Becher, the anthology was burned.
Although some of the pieces had been written by a fourteen year old Byron its material was deemed to be too provocative and passionate.

His collection *Hours of Idleness* followed, it received a harsh critique from an anonymous source who was thought to have been Henry Peter Brougham of the Edinburgh Review who would go on to pursue a career in law and serve as a Whig Lord Chancellor.

Byron wrote a satirical work in response to his detractors titled *English Bards and Scotch Reviewers,* he did not add his name to the piece but it was widely attributed to him.

To be singled out by Byron when he'd achieved great fame became like a badge of honour but at that time it did not have the same effect, he was challenged to a duel by a critic instead.

Byron took his seat in the House of Lords on 13th March 1809 and he received praise for advocating social reform.

Three months later Byron travelled to Europe.

Napoleon Bonaparte was waging war across most of the continent so he stayed in the Mediterranean countries, Spain, Portugal, Albania and Greece for much of the time.

Perhaps Byron hoped to expand his homosexual experiences, to avoid the attentions of Mary Chaworth or it could simply have been the lure of the Islamic countries and his fascination with them that led to him spending three years away from Britain.

He appears to have had an affair with the fourteen year old Nicolo Giraud in Athens, he later sent the young man to a monastery in Malta.

Byron bequeathed seven thousand pounds sterling to Nicolo Giraud in his will but a later version showed no such provision for his former conquest so we have to assume that Nicolo received nothing.

He wrote *Maid of Athens, ere we part* for Teresa Makri, a twelve year old girl. He reputedly offered five hundred pounds (sterling) for her but this was refused.

It is clear to see that in his youth Byron not only experimented with homosexuality but that he had a great interest in adolescent boys.

What he intended to do with Teresa Makri is unknown.

When he returned to England in 1812 he sent a poem to his literary agent for publication.

Byron had no great expectations for the work and there was nothing to suggest that he would become the star of Regency England almost overnight, even before the work was released in its entirety.

Childe Harold's Pilgrimage was published in four instalments and from the first canto (instalment) it received monumental praise.

The great and the good wished to meet him and to have Byron grace their social gatherings. He was hastily inducted in to several exclusive clubs and he dazzled his many admirers who flocked around him.

Lord Byron's star was firmly in the assent.

Mad, Bad And Dangerous To Know

The twenty six year old Lady Caroline Lamb met Lord George Byron at a gathering at Holland House in London in early March 1812.

She'd previously refused to be introduced to him at a ball given by Lady Jersey although she had been intrigued enough to read an advance copy of *Childe Harold's Pilgrimage*.

She'd referred to Byron as *"mad, bad and dangerous to know."*

During their first meeting Byron was encircled by admiring women, Caroline was the exception, she remained aloof.

She wrote to him on the 9th and 11th March to offer her compliments and to urge him not to waste his talents, she also composed a poetic response to *Childe Harold* and imitated

Byron's writing style.

In today's terms, she was writing fan mail.

Byron did not normally take time to reply to his adoring public but when he learned that Lady Caroline Lamb was the author of the letters he wrote back.

They continued to correspond and quite often several letters a day would be exchanged.

During their affair they wrote approximately three hundred letters although very few of them have survived.

Byron pursued her for several reasons, she was physically different to his usual type of conquest, she did not fall at once in to his arms, she was the niece of the famed Georgiana, Duchess of Devonshire and she was known to behave outrageously.

Caroline was bored in her marriage and she craved attention and excitement, an affair was the perfect antidote to tedious days.

For a while Byron was mesmerised by her

It was more than a physical liaison. It was a meeting of minds.

Byron described her as *"the cleverest most agreeable, absurd,*

amiable, perplexing, dangerous fascinating little being..." in a

letter to her written in April 1812.

He gave her the name of "Caro" which she adopted publicly as

a nickname.

They had many common interests, they loved animals, both

enjoyed music, singing and writing songs, Caroline matched

him in wit and he admired her determination to care for her

son at home.

Politically they agreed with one another, although Caroline as

William's wife had assisted and campaigned with him for the

Whig Party she had grown critical of the hypocrisy of their

lifestyle, as had Byron.

Dancing was an area in which they disagreed. Byron's club foot hindered him and Caroline loved to dance, particularly the waltz. She often sat beside him and watched the dancing rather than incite his jealous rage by accepting another dance partner.

As they pursued their clandestine affair and spoke in whispers of love for one another they were careful to be dismissive or rude about each another in society. Their efforts fooled no one, their affair was the talk of polite society.

Byron stimulated Caroline and he gave her a new role in life, of a passionate and desirable creature, but his interest in her soon shifted to a quest to see how much damage she was willing to cause to her marriage and reputation.
He pressured her to confess that she loved him more than William and he hinted that they might elope although it was

never his intention to do so, such discussions were a test of her devotion to him.

In August 1812 Caroline fled the Lamb's home, she was found and Byron returned her to her husband at Brocket Hall.

Her mother, Henrietta, was said to have collapsed with the effect of the scandal and Caroline was taken to the Bessborough estates in Ireland to prevent any further ill advised actions.

William Lamb was as supportive of his wife as he could be under the circumstances but his mother, Elizabeth, Viscountess Melbourne, was less disposed to be so.

Elizabeth had grown to dislike her daughter in law intensely since she had embarrassed the Lamb family with the Sir Godfrey Webster affair.

To Elizabeth, Byron's arrival in Caroline's life had been a heaven sent reason to encourage William to separate from her and to take sole custody of their son. She believed that Caroline brought her troubles upon herself and that she was harmful to William's political career.

Ironically, it was the scandal surrounding Caroline and Byron that brought William Lamb to the attention of all, including powerful politicians.

Byron's confidante at the time of his affair with Caroline was Elizabeth Lamb so it can only be imagined what he told her as time passed.

William was dismayed that his mother and Byron had conspired against Caroline and he branded Byron treacherous.

Caroline would have happily remained in Ireland, she refused to believe that the object of her ardent affection would not eventually elope with her.

She could be forgiven for her misplaced faith in him.

As she left for Ireland he wrote to her that no one "...*shall ever hold the place in my affection which is...most sacred to you till I am nothing."*

Byron and Caroline continued to write letters to one another for her first month of exile but it became a one sided correspondence thereafter until she received two letters from him with his new lover, Lady Oxford's, seal on them.
He told her that he was no longer hers and that she should *"...exert your absurd caprices upon another and leave me in peace."*

Lady Caroline suffered a nervous breakdown and at Christmas 1812 she burned his letters and an effigy of him in a fire as local children stood around her and recited a poem that she'd written which compared Byron to Guy Fawkes.

This was just the start, the imaginative Byron would not have dared to suspect what would happen when she returned to London in 1813.

Public Outbursts And Private Woes

Lady Caroline Lamb's emotional state regarding Byron and his rejection of her grew to such an obsessive level that psychiatrists could have diagnosed a condition called erotomania, which in simple terms is a fixation with a famous person where you believe that they love you.

The high profile person's denial or refusal of love for the sufferer is perceived as an effort to conceal the forbidden love from the world while secret communication is imagined via telepathy, body language and covert signals.
The sufferer sends gifts and seeks out the object of their obsession as if their affection was being returned.

With this illness, Caroline went to exceptional lengths to try to keep Byron in her life.

She wrote anonymously to John Murray II, his publisher, to obtain Byron's picture.

She dressed as a pageboy (she liked the anonymity that dressing as a male gave to her) to gain access to Byron's home and she loitered outside of building's that were hosting events that he was expected to attend.

She also sent him some cuttings of her pubic hair in a letter.

On one of her successful attempts to gain access to Byron's home she wrote *"Remember me!"* in one of his books.

He responded to this with a hateful poem which included the line *"Remorse and shame shall cling to thee..."*

Her most infamous public display was at Lady Heathcote's ball on the 5th July 1813.

Caroline came face to face with Byron, not for the first time, but this event was a waltzing party and of course, dancing had caused friction between them before.

She said that she supposed that she was free to dance again and he rather scornfully replied that she could dance with everyone. His inference being that he no longer cared for her and a jealous reaction would not be forthcoming.

A humiliated Caroline smashed a glass and attempted to slash her wrists, thankfully she did not harm herself greatly and it is doubtful that she intended to kill herself but her public outburst led people to question her sanity.

Byron was less than sympathetic towards her, he labelled the display as a theatrical performance.

The incident was reported in the newspapers so any hopes of containing the situation were swiftly quashed.

In the October of 1813 she contacted John Murray II with a proposition that he should publish "250 Letters from a Venetian nobleman addrest (sic) to a very absurd English lady."

The offer was declined, Byron was informed and he remained forever concerned about what Caroline might publish relating to him.

Caroline's Spencer grandmother died on 18th March 1814, she had been a large part of her life and the emotional effect must have been enormous on an already overwrought woman.

Her friends were unsettled by her, notably Harryo, her close childhood friend and Devonshire cousin.

She paid a visit to Caroline in December 1816 and was so shocked by her behaviour that she decided to make her calls far less frequent.

Byron had established that he needed to marry a wealthy woman to pay off his numerous debts.

He pursued the daughter of Sir Ralph and the Honourable Lady Judith Milbanke, and the niece of Elizabeth, Viscountess Melbourne.

Born on 17th May 1792, Annabella (Anne Isabella) Milbanke was an intelligent and religious woman.

She did not conceal her love of philosophy or mathematics.

Byron called her the Princess of Parallelograms.

In turn, she coined the term Byromania.

They met in March 1812 at around the same time that he was introduced to Caroline.

Annabella refused his amorous advances that spring but after his affair with Caroline he set about capturing her heart.

From August 1813 they began to correspond and Sir Ralph Milbanke invited Byron to visit the family seat at Seaham Hall in County Durham.

In October 1812 Byron proposed to Annabella but she refused him, although she was undeniably enthralled by him.

Another scandal surrounded Byron, this time it concerned his half sister, Augusta, from "Mad Jack's" first marriage.

When Augusta gave birth to a daughter, Elizabeth Medora, on 15th April 1814 there were rumours that her father was not her husband, Colonel George Leigh, but Byron and that made her the product of an incestuous relationship.

As the gossip circulated, Byron determinedly focused on securing a marriage to Annabella.

In September 1814 Byron proposed again and he was accepted.

They married at Seaham Hall on 2nd January 1815 in a private ceremony; the vicar that carried out the service was her illegitimate cousin, Reverend Thomas Noel.

Lord and Lady Byron returned to London and lived in Piccadilly Terrace.

Their union floundered quickly and spectacularly.

Byron was still in acute financial difficulties despite his marriage and he could not find any buyers for his properties. He started to drink in excess, his mood was generally sour and he was vile to his wife.

He was sure that Annabella searched his desk in his absence; she began to worry that he was going mad.

Annabella fell pregnant, Byron was fascinated with Augusta Leigh and by the autumn of 1815 he was having an affair with a chorus girl named Susan Boyce.

That November Augusta Leigh offered to stay at the house to help a heavily pregnant Annabella cope with Byron, she too had noticed that there was something seriously amiss.

On 10th December the only child of their marriage, the Honourable Augusta Ada Byron, to be known as Ada, was born.

Her father's melancholy and anger increased with her arrival.

In January 1816 Annabella arranged for a physician to call at Piccadilly Terrace so that he could confirm if Byron was insane.

She contacted John Hanson, Byron's solicitor, to whom she related her fear that her husband might commit suicide and she fled her home with her baby and took refuge with her parents Sir Ralph and Lady Judith Milbanke.

Her parents sought an official separation for her, Annabella never saw her husband again although she wrote him some warm letters.

When the legal documents stating the details of a separation reached Piccadilly Terrace Augusta Leigh did not show them to Byron, she was too frightened that he might take his own life.

She returned the papers to Annabella but the following week they arrived at Piccadilly Terrace again, Augusta had no choice but to show them to her half brother.

Byron refused to accept that the marriage was over until Annabella used his homosexual relationships and his numerous other misdemeanours as leverage.

The Byron's separation became legal in the March of 1816, just fourteen months after they had married.

Caroline's loyalties were divided, she defended Byron against the charges levelled by his wife but she was jealous of her.

She supported Annabella's quest to have sole custody of Ada while allegedly she provided Byron with lovers.

Annabella was resigned to the fact that she had been unable to save him from himself.

She made records of their relationship lest he should try to gain custody of Ada.

As she grew, Ada was watched closely to ensure that she did not develop her father's unsavoury habits but she was quite rebellious, a Byron trait.

Byron left England that spring.

Lady Caroline and Glenarvon

Caroline's novel *Glenarvon* was published by Henry Colburn in 1816, only weeks after Byron had left the country. Caroline had spent one month writing it before she'd offered it to Byron's publisher John Murray II, he'd declined it.

Henry Colburn had no divided loyalties and he would have recognised the opportunity to make a great deal of money from the work of such an infamous character.

Although it was released anonymously it was widely known that Lady Caroline Lamb was the author and the bones of the plot only served to confirm this.

Glenarvon was set during the Irish Rebellion and it featured infanticide and murder but primarily it was a colourful account of her affair with Lord Byron.

The characters could be easily matched to their real counterparts and several members of Regency society were not pleased to see themselves in the work.

Viscount and Viscountess Melbourne had a doctor confirm that their daughter in law was insane and their son William almost deserted his wife but he endured the great humiliation and he reputedly supported Caroline's writing career.

Lady Jersey cancelled Caroline's vouchers at Almack's Assembly Rooms, a limited membership social venue open to only the finest men and women in society, and Caroline found herself excluded from gatherings that she would formerly have frequented.

Lady Cowper, her sister in law, did manage to get Caroline back in to Almack's in 1819 although the scandal that travelled with her meant that she was never happily accepted in high society again.

In the book, Lady Calantha Delaval, the daughter of the Duke of Altamonte, does not marry her cousin William Buchanan as expected, she falls in love with the Earl of Avondale and they are married.

Calantha loves her husband but she finds herself attracted to the Earl of Glenarvon, who has recently returned from Italy. Glenarvon and Calantha have a passionate affair that causes a scandal.

Both characters die, Calantha firstly, in her outwardly forgiving husband's presence, full of guilt and remorse.

The Earl of Glenarvon eventually drowns after a number of torturous memories of the women that he has ill used and the suffering that he has caused fill his mind.

The spirit of a radiant Calantha appears to him and he asks if she still loves him. Her form becomes careworn and pained. He has his answer and he is condemned in the afterlife.

Caroline's book sold very well, three editions were released in as many months, French and Spanish versions were produced and financially all concerned were happy with the venture. Byron's opinion of the book when he read it was reputedly "...*God damn!*" which was a short comment that spoke volumes.

In my opinion the critics who have branded *Glenarvon* to be unreadable are too harsh but it is an exhausting read, melodramatic in the extreme.

I was relieved to finish it.

Perhaps it is not a book that commands literary praise but it communicated what Caroline needed to say, regardless of the ramifications.

She felt and she wrote passionately, her plentiful descriptive words leave the reader with no doubts.

Caroline wrote two works that were clearly meant as comedic reactions to Byron's epic *Don Juan*.

A New Canto was released in 1819 and *Gordon: A tale* followed in 1821.

She followed these in 1822 and 1823 with novels that the reader could assume were inspired by Byron.

The themes of sacrificing morals, neglecting the chances for redemption and banishment to the fires of hell seem to be a commentary on her former lover's life.

Caroline never recovered from the loss of Byron and her writing was a way to excise her pain. She could respond to his words and possibly inspire him to reply to hers.

She mocked, taunted and teased him at her will.

In addition, others would form views on what she had written so she had the power to affect his popularity.

When news of Byron's death reached Caroline she was

shattered by the loss.

She accidentally saw his funeral procession as it passed through Welwyn close to Brocket Hall.

The following year Lady Caroline persuaded William Lamb to agree to a formal separation. By this time both of them had conducted extramarital affairs.

Caroline lived at Brocket Hall. William was given the post of Chief Secretary for Ireland and he made his home there.

Caroline wrote nothing significant after Byron's death.

Her last years were consumed with battling her mental health problems, alcohol addiction and her use of laudanum.

By 1827 a full time doctor was in attendance upon her.

She grew frailer and when she developed dropsy her life ebbed away without protest.

William made the voyage from Ireland to be by her bedside and on 26th January 1828 she died.

He was deeply affected by the loss of his wild but tragic wife.

Lord Byron - A Poetic Ending

When Byron, accompanied by his physician John W. Polidari, left England in April 1816 he travelled through Belgium, up the Rhine and then he resided for a time at Villa Diodati which sat by Lake Geneva in Switzerland.

He formed friendships with the poet Percy Bysshe Shelley and his future wife Mary Godwin who would achieve fame as Mary Shelley.

Mary's stepsister, Claire Clairmont was staying with them.

Due to awful weather in June 1816 a great deal of literary work was completed by these creative souls.

Mary wrote *Frankenstein,* Polidori wrote *The Vampyre* and Byron worked on the third canto of *Childe Harold's Pilgrimage.*

All of the party read extensively.

Byron spent the winter of 1816-17 in Venice, there he fell in love with his landlady, the married Marianna Segati.
She was quickly succeeded by another mistress, the twenty two year old married Marianna Cogni.

She boldly left her husband and moved in with Byron.
Their intense arguments regularly caused Byron to sleep on his gondola rather than in his home.
When he asked Marianna to go she threw herself in to the canal.

Byron relocated to Rome before returning to Venice to write the fourth canto of *Childe Harold's Pilgrimage*.
He sold Newstead Abbey in 1817 which must have been welcome and long awaited news.

Claire Clairmont gave Byron an illegitimate daughter, born in Bath, England on 12th January 1817 named Clara Allegra (originally she was Alba, Claire's nickname for Byron had been Albé.)

Byron's ardour had cooled towards Claire.

He had moved on to Ravenna where he fell in love again, this time with Countess Teresa Guiccioli.

Byron was so enamoured that he would have eloped with her but, predictably, she was already married. He remained in the town to be close to her.

Shelley visited him during his time there.

He recorded that Byron's home contained a menagerie of animals. Among them there were eight dogs, five cats, five peacocks, ten horses and a falcon.

Byron learned a new language, Armenian, and he studied the country's culture. This led to his co-operation with two books on English and Armenian grammar and a dictionary published between 1817 and 1821.

Between 1818 and 1822 he wrote twelve cantos of his epic work *Don Juan.*

Shelley and Byron with another man, Leigh Hunt, started a newspaper, *The Liberal* but it was a short lived venture.

Clara Allegra, his daughter with Claire Clairmont, died of a fever aged just five years old on 20th April 1822.

From the age of fifteen months old Byron had provided care for her either with people that he chose or at a Roman Catholic convent.

His interest in her had wavered during her short life.

On 8th July 1822 Percy Bysshe Shelley and another friend died in a boating accident.

Byron moved to Genoa with Countess Guiccioli and the Earl and Countess of Blessington.

The Countess later wrote a book titled *Conversations with Lord Byron* which recounted this period.

Byron became bored.

He sold his yacht, Bolivar, to the Earl and Countess of Blessington and hired the boat Hercules to take him to Greece so that he could help the population to gain independence from the Ottoman Empire.

The journey took from 16th July to the 4th August and during this brief spell Byron found time to pursue his Greek page, Lukas Chalandritsanos.

He arrived in Missolonghi, Western Greece on 29th December and joined with the politician Mavrokordatos.

On 15th February 1824 Byron fell ill and the normal medical treatment of bloodletting was employed but it only weakened the patient.
He rallied slightly before he caught a strong cold which was treated with more bloodletting.
This aggravated his condition.

Quite probably dirty or unsterilized medical equipment was the cause of Byron contracting the violent fever and sepsis from which he did not survive.
Byron died on 19th April 1824 aged thirty six.

It was claimed by some that if Byron had lived he might have been proclaimed the King of Greece.

The Greeks did mourn his loss deeply and he was a hero to them.

"Vyron" the Greek form of Byron became a popular boys name and a town near to Athens was called Vyronas in his honour.

Byron's heart remained in Missolonghi but the rest of his corpse was embalmed and returned to a shocked England.

It was hoped that he would be buried in Westminster Abbey but the request to carry this out was refused with Byron's "questionable morality" proving to be an immovable obstacle to the Church.

He lay in state in London for two days where eager crowds gathered to view him.

He was then taken to Nottinghamshire and buried at the Church of St. Mary Magdalene in Hucknall.

In a remarkable tribute the Greek King sent a marble slab to be placed above Byron's grave.

A duplicate of this slab was eventually accepted and placed in Westminster Abbey.

It was not until 1969 that Byron received a memorial in the Abbey.

Byron's friends raised £1000 for the creation of a statue of him.

It was completed in 1834 but St. Paul's Cathedral, Westminster Abbey and the National Gallery were among the establishments that refused to house it.

Byron's statue eventually went to the library at Trinity College, Cambridge.

His portraits, on his orders, did not show him as a writer, pen in hand, but as an adventurer, a man who lived life fully.

This is how he must have wished to be remembered.

The Byron's, Lambs and Former Conquests

Byron's barony was inherited by his cousin, a naval officer named George Anson Byron.

Today the title is held by the 13th Baron, Robert Byron, born in 1950.

He is the president of the British Byron Society.

In 1832 John Murray II released Byron's complete works which incorporated a biography by Byron's friend Thomas Moore.

Popular, another edition was published the following year.

Don Juan was acclaimed as one of the most important epic poems since John Milton's *Paradise Lost*.

Lady Annabella Byron became committed to social causes and she was a key figure at the World Anti Slavery Convention in 1840.

She inherited the title of Baroness Wentworth from her maternal uncle but she chose not to use it as she was widely known as Baroness (Lady) Byron.

Annabella died on 16th May 1860 from breast cancer.

As she lay dying she imparted her version of her stormy marriage to the American writer Harriet Beecher Stowe (1811-1896.)

The author was Annabella's fierce advocate, letters were reproduced that confirmed Byron's worsening drunkenness in 1815-16 and his brutal treatment of his wife and these were added to the assertion that the rumoured incest between

Byron and Augusta Leigh had been confirmed by Byron himself.

Augusta had taken pains to decry such talk as insane ramblings to Annabella.

Lady Byron Vindicated was published in 1869 and it was hugely damaging to the long deceased Byron's reputation.

Lady Byron was buried in Kensal Green Cemetery in London, hundreds of miles away from the body of her husband.

The Honourable Augusta Ada Byron worked with the mathematician, inventor and engineer Charles Babbage (1791-1871) and she is considered by many to be the world's first computer programmer because she wrote the first algorithm for Babbage's analytical engine machine.

She had a keen understanding of how humans and technology could work together.

Ada married William, the eighth Baron King, later 1st Earl of Lovelace and she had three children, Byron, Anne Isabella and Ralph Gordon.

Countess Ada Lovelace died on 27th November 1852 from cancer.

She was thirty six years old, the same age that her father had been at the time of his death.

She was laid to rest beside him at the graveyard in Hucknall, Nottinghamshire.

Her mother survived her by eight years.

Augusta Leigh lived until 12th October 1851, she was unhappily married, bore seven children and was left in debt thanks to her husband's gambling. She survived him by approximately a year.

Elizabeth Medora Leigh, Byron and Augusta's alleged

daughter, died on 28th August 1849 aged thirty five years old.
She had led a troubled life abundant with affairs and two
illegitimate children. She married the father of her second
child, Jean-Louis Taillefer, on 23rd August 1848 and her death
came five days after her first wedding anniversary.

Her daughter Marie Violette became a nun and her son Elie
became a priest.

Caroline became known to history as Lady Caroline Lamb
rather than Melbourne because she died before William
inherited the title from his father.

William, the 2nd Viscount Melbourne, rose through the
political ranks to become the British Prime Minister in 1834
and between 1835 -1841. He served and closely advised Queen
Victoria during the first years of her long reign.

He was linked to sexual scandals and in 1836 when his close
friend, the author and feminist Caroline Norton left her violent

husband George who unsuccessfully attempted to blackmail Lamb - he alleged that William and Caroline had committed adultery and indulged in criminal conversation - it could have ruined him but it appears that the respect of his colleagues secured his career and standing in society.

The Lamb's son, George Augustus, lived for twenty nine years and he was given as full a life as possible.

His final hours were spent lying on a sofa as his father worked in the same room, he appeared to be asleep but he suddenly and quietly commented that it was a shame that he had no stamps (franks) so that he could write and thank people for their inquiries about him.

Again, he became silent and a few hours later he expired.

Lord Melbourne died on 24th November 1848 and his titles passed to his brother Frederick, he died childless in 1853.

Melbourne Hall was bestowed on their sister Lady Emily

Cowper but the titles became extinct.

Claire Clairmont, Clara Allegra Byron's mother died on 19th March 1879 in Florence, Italy aged eighty.

She survived her stepsister Mary Shelley by twenty eight years.

Countess Teresa Guiccioli lived between 1800 and 1873.

Alexandre Dumas based a character in *The Count of Monte Cristo* on her.

John Murray II died in 1843.

He had enjoyed an extensive publishing career. His stable of authors included Jane Austen. Sir Walter Scott and Samuel Taylor Coleridge.

His descendant, John Murray IV, was Queen Victoria's publisher.

Bessborough House in Roehampton is now called Parkstead House and it sits in the grounds of Roehampton University.

Melbourne House in London is the The Albany, an apartment complex.

Melbourne Hall, Brocket Hall and Newstead Abbey are open to the public.

Lord George Byron and Lady Caroline Lamb were two intriguing Regency characters. They live on in their work and in biographies and the tale of their relationship is still compelling.

In places it's tragic, in others spectacular or brutal.

They proved that there was indeed a thin line between love and hate.

Images

Lady Caroline Lamb.

Lord George Byron.

Newstead Abbey in the mid nineteenth century.

Circa 1830 – Melbourne House in London. Today it is an apartment block, The Albany.

Lady Annabella (Anne Isabella) Byron.

Augusta Leigh.

William Lamb, the 2ⁿᵈ Viscount Melbourne in later life.

Ada, Countess of Lovelace –

Byron's daughter from his marriage and his only

legitimate child.

Thank you for reading this book.

If you enjoyed it please spread the word.

More of my books are available from Amazon and other online retailers.

My short stories are available on www.alfiedog.com and a selection of my children's stories have been published on www.childrens-stories.net

My website is at www. joannehayle.co.uk

I also have a positive blog about O.C.D.,P.T.S.D. and my writing: joannehayle.wordpress.com

Thank you

Joanne.

www.ingramcontent.com/pod-product-compliance
Lightning Source LLC
Chambersburg PA
CBHW070051240225
22445CB00013B/1122